It began early in the night of the 5th and 6th June when paratroops landed. In the small hours, following intense bombing, landings began, co-ordinated to the flow of the incoming tide. Westward, the first two sectors were allocated to the 1st American Army Utah (Sainte-Marie-du-Mont) and Omaha (Pointe du Hoc - Colleville). In the East : 2nd British Army landed on the beaches between Bayeux and Caen. Between the two British sectors : Gold (Arromanches) and Sword (Lion-sur-Mer - Ouistreham) the Canadians landed on Juno (Courseulles - Langrune).

By the evening of 6th June, five bridgeheads had been established somewhat strained and still fragile after bloody skirmishes. Each side had lost nearly 10,000 men (killed, wounded, missing or taken prisoner). In the days that followed, burying the Dead was a primary factor. The first of these were assembled and buried behind the lines as the troops moved inland. The first cemeteries were provisional and sited near the landing beaches, such as Sainte-Mère-Église (near Utah), Vierville (Omaha), Bény-sur-Mer (Juno) or Hermanville (Sword). The Fallen of both sides were assembled and interred not far apart.

The British Cemeteries indicate some of the first engagements

In the British sector the Front advanced slowly between Bayeux, freed on 7th June and Caen, not until 18th July. The British and Canadians were held up outside Caen by strong German resistance. Every hamlet, field, hedge even, meant several days of fighting. The wounded were evacuated promptly. The dead were interred provisionally and removed later when a lull in action made it possible. It was the task of the Royal Army Chaplains Dept to minister to the Dying, and to bury the Dead whether friend or foe.

Numbers of provisional cemeteries sprang up in the wake of the advancing troops, often near Field Hospitals or near villages in the hands of British or Canadian Forces. Very many of the Commonwealth war Graves to the norh and west of Caen that are dotted across the countryside today, trace the route and hardship of the British 2nd Army in its advance towards Caen.

In the Foreground, the first casualties. In the background, an LST about to come in-shore.

The great American provisional cemeteries

In the American sector after the murderous onslaughts of Omaha and Utah, the days that followed proved no less difficult. The celebrated "Hedge-war" began. The American advance slowed down but casualties were just as high. Up to the end of July there was fierce fighting in the Cotentin where armour and infantry intermingled in a serried web of thicket and woodland where danger stalked behind each hedge and rise. From the start the U.S. Army had units detailed specially to take charge of the Fallen as the troops advanced. Friend and foe were then interred in provisional grave-yards.

Sites were chosen that corresponded to certain criteria : primarily of easy access, (as roads were often teeming with army transport) on well-drained high ground where the bodies would not quickly decompose (since they might have to be moved later) and finally light soil that could be trenched easily, five feet deep (1m50) where the Dead, buried in sacks, were aligned. A wooden cross or just a stake with a helmet marked each grave. Many German soldiers were buried without marked graves and exhumed very much later.

The German "Armour Ace" Michael Wittman was only found in 1983 at Cintheaux under the verge at the roadside, forty centimetres down. Every year bodies are found in fields and apple-orchards.

WHILE THE BATTLE RAGED

The provisional American Cemetery at St Laurent in 1944

The Battle nears its end

With Cherbourg freed, American troops on 31st July pressed on to Brittany through the Avranches Gap. The speed of their advance allowed them also to attack eastwards to Mortain where they repulsed a German counter-attack, and to advance in Mayenne and the Sarthe where Enemy forces were fewer. Two more cemeteries were added : Saint James, following the break-through at Avranches and Chêne-Guérin near Percy, following the fighting around Vire and Mortain. In the latter, graves were dug for both friend and foe. British Forces got through to Vire in the first week of August and laid out a cemetery at Saint-Charles-de-Percy.

On 12th August, General Leclerc liberated Alençon with the French Forces under his command, closing the Falaise Pocket where two German armies divisions were hemmed in. Americans to the south, British on the west, Canadian and Polish troops to the north and east, routed, then finally annihilated the last German resistance in Normandy. At Chambois on 21st August the Battle of Normandy ended. German Units that had escaped, fell back towards the Seine. The last British engagements were along the Touques as far as Lisieux and Orbec and the Americans around Evreux. Two new cemeteries were set up at Saint-Désir-de-Lisieux (British and German) ; and another in the Eure at Champigny-Saint-André (American and German). Paris was liberated a few days later. Thus began a new phase that led the Allies to the gates of Germany itself.

The toll is heavy

When the Battle of Normandy ended if most of the Fallen were in provisional cemeteries, laid out by the Allied Armies, many other graves, alone or in groups still dotted the countryside. Churchyards too had received the bodies

of the warriors. Today there are still over two hundred lone graves or squares of tombs of French and British soldiers, buried either after a skirmish or in the days and months that preceded the Battle (Airmen, Commandos, Paras). Many disappeared in the heat of the battle : aircrew and seamen who fell into the sea, infantrymen buried during action, mutilated corpses hastily covered over.

Over 100,000 soldiers of thirteen nationalities repose forever in the soil of Normandy : 13,800 Americans (2,055 missing), 17,000 British (1,808 missing in the Army alone), 5,110 Canadians, 729 Poles, 246 French, 27 Australians, 19 New Zealanders, 7 South Africans, 7 Russians, 3 Czechs, 2 Italians, 2 Belgians… and over 70,000 Germans.

MAPS - The battle and the cemeteries

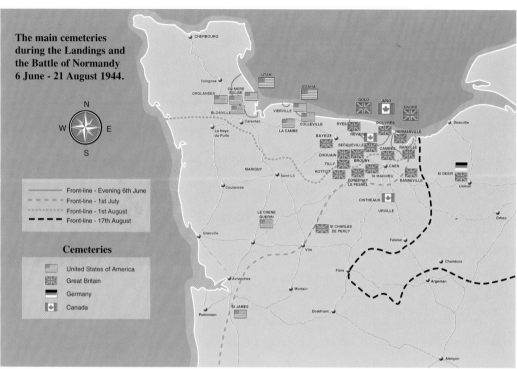

The main cemeteries during the Landings and the Battle of Normandy 6 June - 21 August 1944.

Front-line - Evening 6th June
Front-line - 1st July
Front-line - 1st August
Front-line - 17th August

Cemeteries

- United States of America
- Great Britain
- Germany
- Canada

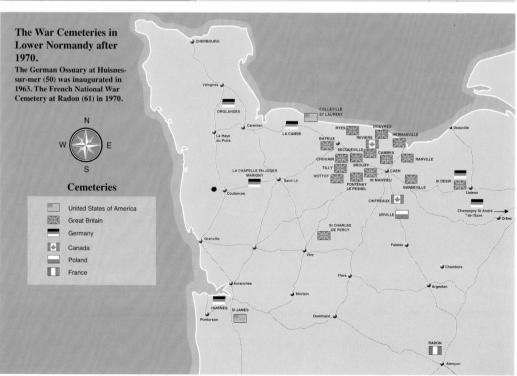

The War Cemeteries in Lower Normandy after 1970.

The German Ossuary at Huisnes-sur-mer (50) was inaugurated in 1963. The French National War Cemetery at Radon (61) in 1970.

Cemeteries

- United States of America
- Great Britain
- Germany
- Canada
- Poland
- France

After the war : the regrouping of graves

At the end of the Second World War, there were several hundred provisional cemeteries, 24 of which were in France, laid out by the American Graves Registration, an ancillary service of the U.S. Army. About ten cemeteries were in Lower Normandy : Vierville, Colleville, Saint-Laurent, two at Sainte-Mère-Église, Blosville, La Cambe, Orglandes, Marigny, Saint-James and Le-Chêne-Guérin.

It was in 1947 that fourteen sites worldwide were chosen as permanent cemeteries for American soldiers. The choice of site bore reference to a glorious feat of arms nearby in the Second World War. For each of these an architect was to design a non-confessional chapel, a wall to commemorate the missing, a museum containing battle-maps and a visitors' hall as well as a war memorial. In the same year, France and the United States governments signed an Agreement regarding the setting up of five permanent cemeteries on French soil. Between 1947 and 1954, the American Graves registration repatriated the bodies of 172,000 soldiers to the USA at the request of their families ; 14,000 of these were from Normandy.

In Lower Normandy, two historic sites were decided on : Colleville-sur-Mer at Omaha "The Bloody", the first of the Allied Landings in Northern Europe and at Saint-James in the Manche where at one time General Patton had his Command-post, a symbol of the Avranches Break-out. In 1956 the government of France granted to the United States rights of the lands in and around the cemeteries and monuments.

The American Battle Monuments Commission was created by an act of Congress in March 1923. It is responsible for everything concerning monuments and memorials commemorating the American Armed Forces who fell in battle on foreign soil. This is an independent agency of the executive branch of the United States Government, although financed by the US Government. The Superintendent in charge of each cemetery is an American citizen.

These two cemeteries are well organised to welcome visitors with personnel always available to give information and maintain supervision. They are the only cemeteries in Lower Normandy with definite visiting hours. Colleville in particular has a touristic element as shown by its large parking areas for cars and coaches. It is said to have nearly two million visitors a year. Droves of tourists arrive in coaches attracted by the way in which one nation has honoured its Fallen in the cause of Freedom. A large expanse around the Memorial has been left for ceremonies and parades beneath flags flying on very tall masts. The Commemoration is a striking reminder of one generation sacrificed for another.

THE AMERICAN CEMETERIES

From 1947 onwards, the bodies of soldiers buried in the provisional cemeteries nearest to Colleville were taken there by the American Army. In March 1948, the graves from three cemeteries near Sainte-Mère-Église were removed, amongst which was that of General Theodore Roosevelt.

The architects, Harbeson, Livigston and Larson, as well as Stevenson a landscape gardener, all from Philadelphia, were given the task of laying out the cemetery, the memorial and 173 acres of ground overlooking the Landing Beaches. After four years in construction it was finished in 1956, given the name of the Normandy American Cemetery and inaugurated on 19th July of the same year.

On the field of conflict

Situated on a plateau overlooking Omaha Beach the grave-yard is a vast rectangle parallel to the shore. The land put at the disposal of the United States, stretched right down to the beach for about a kilometre in length and six hundred metres wide. It included also, the way from the 'Route Departementale' up to the Cemetery gates. No one enters Colleville Cemetery by chance, one has to make one's way there.

It is a vast majestic park, making the most of its position and the surprise effect. The sea, framed between a double row of evergreen oaks draws the visitor to the focal point. The eye ranges over the immense green carpet studded with white crosses in faultless lines. Over to the west is the other sea, towards the United States : space, the sound of the wind, the sea, all is there… the soul takes flight. From entering, right up to the balcony overlooking the sea, the effect is all-embracing with an innate abundance which the architects have heightened to great effect. The accent is on a site to glorify a great nation. It is a place for the victorious, a place of glory to the memory of fallen heroes.

Colleville - St Laurent

The symbolism of the Memorial

The entire layout of the site is determined by the majestic central mall on which the monuments are arranged. At the eastern end of the main axis stands the Memorial, a spacious construction - two loggias linked by a semi-circular colonnade which is reflected in a rectangular pool. The whole symbolises an opportunity for future generations of remembrance and reunion. In the centre of the Memorial at the axis of the mall a bronze statue seven metres high symbolises the soul of American youth emerging from the waves. Around the plinth can be read : "Mine eyes have seen the glory of the coming of the Lord". The work is that of the sculptor Donald de Lue of New-York. The terrace between the loggias is studded with shingle from Omaha Beach.

The Memorial is built of limestone from Vaurion in the Côte d'Or, the plinths and the steps are in granite from Ploumanach in Brittany. Beneath the blue ceramic ceilings in the two loggias are maps and explanations of the Battles engraved in the stone. On the south side the largest map traces the 6th June landings from England. On each side two others depict the Naval plan of the Landings and the air operations that preceded it. Three theatres of conflict : Army, Navy and Airforce, where soldiers, sailors and airmen gave their lives. In the North Loggia a gigantic map shows military operations in Western Europe from 6th June 1944 to 8th May 1945. All the Maps have been drawn from the American Battle Monuments Commission documents by Robert Foster.

Two great bronze urns, the work of Donal de Lue flank the entrance of each loggia. Their décor symbolises on the one : War and Death with women and children stricken with grief and misery at the loss of a dear one. The other calls to mind those who perished at sea, the resurrection and Eternal Life. Behind the Memorial, below the terrace, is the garden of the Missing. It forms a semi-circle. The walls are inscribed with the name, rank, unit and State of origin of 1,557 missing servicemen. In central position under the Memorial Colonnade is an extract from the dedication of the Memorial, by General Eisenhower, taken from the "Livre d'Or" kept in Saint Paul's Cathedral in London.

Colleville - St Laurent

Facing the Memorial in the Central Mall, is the Chapel : a circular edifice surrounded by a colonnade. This too is built of Vaurion limestone with steps of granite from Ploumanach. The Frieze above the door carries a copy of the Medal of Honour of the American Congress : the highest and most rare of distinctions awarded for actions of exceptional fame. Within, the altar black and gold, of marble from the Pyrénées, is surrounded by American, French, British and Canadian flags. On the stained-glass window is fixed a fine Latin Cross of teak above a Star of David set within a sun and carrying at its centre a dove. Around the whole are 48 stars representing the United States of America. The ceiling mosaic, the work of Leon Kroll of New York, symbolises America blessing her sons before they depart by sea and by air, whilst France places a crown of laurels on those who gave their lives for the liberation of Europe.

The return of Peace is portrayed by an Angel, a Dove and a Ship coming to land. At the west end of the Central Mall, two statues in Italian granite bearing the Eagle and the Cockerel, depict the United States and France. They are sculptures by Donald de Lue.

Light for dead heroes

From whatever part of the Central mall, the crosses, in squares of ten are impressive : by their faultless alignment and by their dazzling whiteness on the green carpet of lawn. 9,386 American soldiers lie beneath it, four of which are women. 307 of them have never been identified and the inscription reads : "Known but to God". A father and his son lie side by side and in 33 cases two brothers are buried next to each other. They are from every State in the Union and from the District of Columbia with the exception of a few from England, Scotland or Canada. The great majority lost their lives at the time of the Landings or in the liberation of the North Cotentin. Among them are three American Congress Medalists of Honour, one of which is General Theodore Roosevelt, nephew of the President of the United States buried beside his brother Quentin.
(Block D, Row 28, graves 45 & 46)

The memorials in white marble from Lasa in Italy indicate the religion of each soldier : a Star of David for members of the Jewish faith and a Latin cross for Christians. On each is the soldier's name, rank and unit as well as the State he came from and the date of his death. From the Memorial no inscriptions can be seen since the graves face west. The graves bear no distinctive signs or flowers, each one forms a part of the whole, of a great army. All are in strict alignment to the axis of the Central mall, all face west... towards the United States.

A background of sombre green

Of the 173 acres that make up the Concession granted to the United States, the Cemetery takes up about thirty-seven. A large part is laid out as service areas, Visitors' Reception and car-parks. The periphery bordering the surrounding countryside has been planted with trees and shrubs, whilst sea-wards the historic sites down to the beach have retained their character of origin.

Right from the entrance the Cemetery is so arranged that the visitor passes through the various sections in the sequence designed by the architect. A granite gateway flanked with clipped cypress marks the solemnity of the entrance. From this point the drive-in prepares the visitor : a quasi initiation , for entry to the cemetery. The verges are laid to lawn and impeccably kept, whilst the hedge rows are planted with oaks, ash and hawthorn. Normandy still, but one that leads to a different place, another country.

The Southern entrance is between evergreen oaks, trimmed and aligned on a carpet of close-clipped lawn. There are bushes of Eleagnus and Tamaris, then beyond a clump of pines one emerges : with startling surprise - the sea to the north, the beaches where the heroes fell, to the east the impressive Memorial, then the eye falls on the plethora of tombs, a constellation of white crosses on a boundless green carpet stretching to a double row of Austrian Black Pines that mark the limits of the Cemetery.

The woods are a background for the gravestones and encase the monuments, hiving off the Cemetery from its surroundings. They provide a 'mise en scène', creating surprise effects or views beyond : to the north, to the sea and, to the west, towards the church at Vierville.

On the periphery, species of dark evergreen underline the general effect, whilst softer greenery punctuates the central area. This latter is unemcumbered to leave space for the alignment of gravestones. Clumps of conifers and shrubs are dotted among the crosses. Seemingly haphazard, their position so rumour has it, coincides with bomb craters. These were filled with war material, destroyed after 6th June, making burials impossible. Neither floral tributes nor individuality intrudes on the impeccable orderliness and the immense impression of grandeur created. On the eastern side the vegetation is thicker, in harmony with the solemnity of the Memorial. At the axis of the Mall on either side of the basin a double row of evergreen oaks leads up to the Memorial itself. Behind, the Garden of the Missing is more intimate and attuned to silent reflection. Within its half-circle lie four sections of lawn each with an ash-tree and roseborders radiating to the centre of the Memorial. At the foot of the wall on which the names of the Missing are inscribed, St John's Wort and Golden Cypress have been planted.

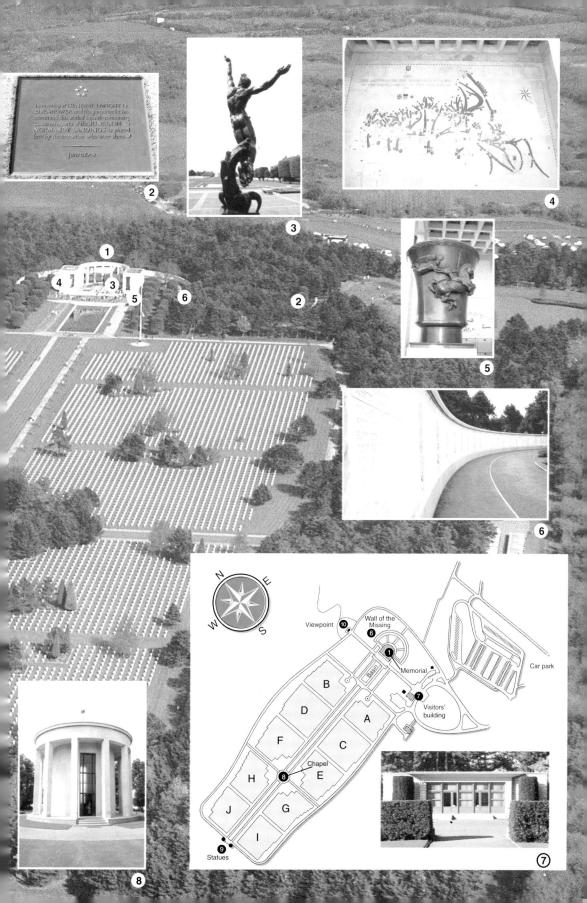

In memory of GENERAL DWIGHT D.
EISENHOWER and the forces under his
command that sealed capsule containing
... news reports of the JUNE 6, 1944 S
NORMANDY LANDINGS is placed
here by the newsmen who were there ...

June 6, 1969

2

3

4

1

4 3

5

6

2

5

6

N
E
W
S

Viewpoint 10 Wall of the
Missing 6

1

Memorial

B

Basin

7

Car park

Visitors'
building

D

A

F

C

H 8 Chapel

E

J G

9 I

Statues

7

8

THE AMERICAN CEMETERIES

Heroes known or unknown…

EISENHOWER, ROOSEVELT,... America and its great men, America and its unnamed heroes, sons from Virginia or elsewhere.

Of the 9,386 soldiers interred at Colleville, three of them received the Congress Medal of Honour, the highest distinction of their Country.

Frank D. PEREGORY did not know on that 8th June in 1944 that he would go down in History for taking part in the liberation of Grandcamp with the 29th Infantry Division. Six days later, Sergeant PEREGORY was killed near Gouvains. He attempted to take a machine-gun nest single-handed.

This act of patriotism and bravery won for him posthumously, recognition from his native land.

Frank PEREGORY was married in 1941. His honeymoon lasted only 2 days.

The State of Virginia was to lose a second son : Jimmie W. MONTEITH 1st U.S. Infantry Division. He landed on Omaha Beach in the first wave of the assault on 6th June. Under a flood of fire and steel he ran up and down the beach, reorganising his men for the next assault. His act of supreme sacrifice was to lead two tanks across minefields and take out several enemy positions.

The story of the ROOSEVELT brothers, nephews of Theodore, President of the United States is marked by a striking co-incidence.

Both died on July but in two different wars. Quentin's plane, he was a Lieutenant in the U.S. Airforce was shot down in the Aisne on 14th July 1918. He is the only soldier of the 1st World War to be buried in Colleville Cemetery.

He was 23.

General Theodore died of a heart attack at the age of 57 on 12th July 1944.

In the Fifties their family decided to reunite them.

First Lieutenant Jimmie W. MONTEITH, Jr.

Theodore ROOSEVELT : Block D, Row 28, Grave 46

Jimmie W. MONTEITH : Block I, Row 20, Grave 12

Men and their stories

There were four of them

Four young Americans joined up in the name of Duty and Patriotism.

Preston, Robert and Francis landed in Normandy in different Units whilst Edward fought in the Pacific as a member of an air-crew.

Robert was killed on 6th June at Sainte-Mère-Église, Preston on 7th at Utah Beach, Edward was reported missing in the same week. The authorities decided then to save the fourth of the NILAND's sons.

The Chaplain, Father Simpson was given the task of breaking the news to the younger son, Francis before evacuating him to England. When the War in the Pacific ended, the airman, a prisoner of the Japanese was finally found again.

It was this moving and incredible story that inspired the scriptwriter of Steven Spielberg for the film : "Saving Private Ryan".

Robert J. NILAND :
Block F, Row 15, Grave 11

Preston T. NILAND :
Block F, Row 15, Grave 12

Men and their stories

Tragic destinies, destinies inter-twined.

The HOBACK brothers of the 29th Infantry Division were killed on the same day at Omaha.

Their company, the first to land at dawn on D-Day was nearly wiped out in 10 minutes.

As soon as he jumped ashore Bradford fell on the sand, killed instantly. His brother Raymond, gravely wounded succombed shortly after. The rising tide carried his body away, leaving amid the horrors of "The Bloody Beach" a bible carefully enclosed in a plastic bag. It was retrieved the day after by a soldier.

Raymond's name is inscribed on the wall of the Missing.

Brothers…

Joseph and Manuel ARRUDA were to have no decorations; they were ordinary soldiers…

The two brothers were in the same landing craft that disgorged its flood of men on Omaha Beach that morning of 6th June. Landing together, they died together after one put his foot on a mine.

Joseph E. ARRUDA :
Block G, Row 9, Grave 25

Manuel E. ARRUDA :
Block G, Row 9, Grave 26

Fathers and sons

Near Saint-Lô on 30th July, Colonel OLLIE's jeep was caught in machine-gun fire. He commanded the 115th Infantry Regiment of the 29th Division.

At the beginning of the same month Lieutenant OLLIE Jr died in the Italian Campaign.

Both father and son were regular serving officers.

Telegrams announcing their deaths were received by their wife and mother within a 45 minute interval.

OLLIE W. REED :
Block E, Row 20, Grave 19

OLLIE W. REED Jr :
Block E, Row 20, Grave 20

Saint James

Another site chosen by the United States as a permanent cemetery in France was Saint James. The choice made, symbolised General Patton's famous Avranches Break-out. The liberation took place on 2nd August and a provisional cemetery was established there three days later. The choice as a permanent site was made on 16th September 1949 and the French Government granted the United States the free use of thirty acres of ground. After the war when the provisional cemeteries were cleared, the American Army regrouped the bodies of 4,410 soldiers to Saint James's. Most of these lost their lives either in the liberation of Saint-Lô or in the Cotentin. The others came from the tip of Brittany to the Seine's east bank. Given the name of Brittany American Cemetery it was inaugurated on 20th July 1956.

A conventional park in the middle of the woods

Dominating the woodland valley between Normandy and Brittany the cemetery of Saint James takes up a sizeable area in rural country. More modest in size than Colleville and without the advantage of such an imposing site, it comprises none the less, all the elements of the "mise en scène" to be found there. On the drive-in the necropolis is hidden from sight right up to the Memorial where the white crosses impeccably aligned rise up from the greensward. Taken at a glance is an expanse westward, the countryside stretching to the sea... the United States. Without doubt, this is the ground of victors : a formal park that a great nation has laid out to honour its sons who fell in battle for a noble cause.

A Norman Church, a place of remembrance

The cemetery of Saint James is laid out on an east-west axis. To the east on the axis of the prospect, a chapel built of granite from Hinglé near Dinan comprises both chapel and museum and forms the Memorial. Architecturally it was designed "with reference to Norman chapels in the region" consisting of a nave and bell-tower thirty metres high from which can be seen Mont-Saint-Michel. As at Colleville, all the aspects of remembrance are found there.

Approaching the Memorial the visitor comes upon a statue of a warrior on horseback slaying a dragon : the triumph of youth over evil. At the other end of the building the entrance is surmounted by two sculptures in granite blocks that symbolise mourning and triumph. Between them, the shield of the United States is surmounted by the American Eagle whilst the thirteen stars of the first States of the Union form an arch. Within are to be found, all that is symbolical of the United States Army and its operations. The stained-glass window at the entrance depicts the emblem of the GHQ of the Allied Expeditionary Forces whilst of those in the Memorial, one portrays the Great Seal of the United States and the others the Arms and features of the eight French towns liberated by the American Army : Carentan, Cherbourg, Saint-Lô, Mont-Saint-Michel, Mortain, Chartres, Paris and Brest. Done in the style of 13th Century stained-glass windows they are the work of F. Lorin of Chartres.

THE AMERICAN CEMETERIES

Sixteen flags of the American Army including that of the Chaplain's Departement hang in different parts of the nave. Above the entrance hang three flags : American, French and British above the motto : "Duty, Honour and Country" which is that of Westpoint. In the museum maps of military operations are displayed on the north and south walls. One concerns the operations on 6th June to the advance to the Seine, the other, operations generally in Western Europe up to 8th May 1945. Six small maps sum up the Key-points of Allied Operations.

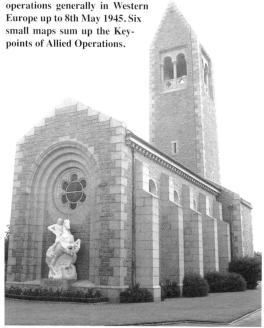

Supporting a terrace, the Wall of the Missing divides off the Memorial from the graves. On the wall are inscribed the names of 498 soldiers the bodies of whom have never been found. At the far end of the cemetery at the axis of the central alley stands a cenotaph, hewn from a single great block of granite on which has been sculptured a torch and crown of laurels with the inscription : "Pro patria 1941-1945".

Saint James

A poise of Peaceful vegetation

Once through the gates an expanse of vegetation prepares the visitor for access to the Memorial itself and its range of grave-stones beyond. Here, across superb lanscaping, the necropolis remains unseen. Close-clipped vegetation is architectural, walls of dark-green holly hedges, low hedges of close-cut box, edge the alleys with topiaried evergreen oaks. Massive clumps of covert and coppice punctuate the drive-ways of this vast park and the Prospect up to the Cenotaph. Gaps appear at some points in the screens of vegetation offering magnificent views of wooded uplands.

The central alley is bordered with Sweet Chestnuts, whilst on the periphery, copses and spinneys are varied : Plantanes, Oak, Beech, Copaifera, Horse Chestnut, Cedar, Yoke-elm, Hawthorn, and even some giant Sequoias.

Like a half-opened fan

An expanse of tombs stretches out from the Memorial. On both sides of the prospect, sixteen squares of stones are arranged concentrically in the form of a half-opened fan. The bodies of 4,410 soldiers are buried here, 97 of which were never identified. There are 95 graves containing the partial remains of different soldiers. In twenty places two brothers lie side by side. The stones are of white marble, quarried in Lasa in Italy. The tombs face west, therefore no inscriptions can be seen from the Memorial. They can only be read when walking up from the east. Amongst the crosses are 81 stones with the Star of David for soldiers of the Jewish Faith. Otherwise there is no distinctive sign, these too form part of a great army lined up here for ever.

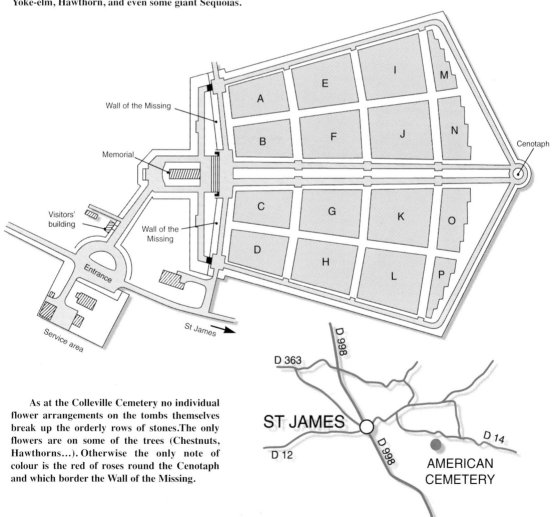

As at the Colleville Cemetery no individual flower arrangements on the tombs themselves break up the orderly rows of stones.The only flowers are on some of the trees (Chestnuts, Hawthorns...). Otherwise the only note of colour is the red of roses round the Cenotaph and which border the Wall of the Missing.

1945

ON WHICH
METERY
THE GIFT
FRENCH
FOR THE
TUAL
PLACE
SAILORS
RS AND
WHO ARE
ED HERE

A soldier lies where he fell

A time-honoured custom of the British Army, has it that a soldier killed in battle is buried in the ground on which he shed his blood. This is why there are 2,500 cemeteries world-wide, some quite small, in 140 different countries. After the Battle of Normandy the Commonwealth War-graves Commission regrouped the graves spread over eighteen cemeteries (sixteen British and two Canadian) laid out along the line of advance. The sixteen cemeteries created are to the north, west and east of Caen. They correspond to the main provisional cemeteries formed in the wake of the Battle. Some were laid-out quite early after the Landings notably : Hermanville and Ryes - Bazenville, others later at Saint-Charles-de-Percy (action near Vire) and at Saint-Désir-de-Lisieux (German retreat towards the Seine).

The body of a British soldier is never repatriated. Often the original burial place is respected. Graves in churchyards are kept sometimes at local request. Thus at Ranville the first soldiers killed, buried in the churchyard have never been transferred to the war-graves nearby. One solitary war-grave at Caumont-l'Éventé receives the same care as those in the War cemeteries. The graves of soldiers of other nationalities are treated with the same respect, not only Allied Forces but those of German soldiers are looked after with the same care as those of the soldiers of the Crown. Of the 979 war-graves at Ryes, 326 are German. The Bayeux Cemetery is the most cosmopolitan with soldiers of eleven nationalities laid to rest there, of which four are from the Commonwealth. Sited originally near a Field Hospital, it was later enlarged to incorporate graves from about fifteen provisional cemeteries between Evrecy and the sea.

From 1945 onwards, after the regrouping of graves the landscaping of the cemeteries began and continued until the beginning of the Fifties. To begin with there were very basic grave-yards with lines of wooden crosses. These were all re-designed in the same way : each soldier was given his own grave-stone. The architects : Sir Hubert Worthington, Philip Hepworth and Sir Edward Mauf, continued the lay-out following a design established in 1917 by The Imperial War Graves Commission. In each cemetery an identical memorial is erected : The Cross of Sacrifice. The Stone of remembrance, an open-air altar is only placed in the larger cemeteries. In Lower Normandy, sixteen British cemeteries became permanent.

There are some 300 Commonwealth graves in the parish churchyards of Lower Normandy most of which are those of pilots and parachutists.

Gardens in sober good taste

Surrounded by low well-trimmed hedges near a road or a village, British cemeteries are gardens, though each an enclave, numerous views are left, of countryside or neigh-bouring township. From afar they melt into the landscape evidenced only from emerging trees silhouetted against the sky-line. Their size, colours and their nature are all that mark their presence. A corner of garden, so close to England yet one senses a strange familiarity. A sentiment not far removed from that entrenched in the veterans them-selves, as they relate the taking or defence of a village or field for their Norman kinsfolk.

The lay-out is simple. Rectangular in shape there is a wide central alley laid to lawn. Stretching from one end to the other it is on this axis that the memorial stone and cross are erected at the intersection of the other alleys, leaving a large space for parades and ceremonial occasions. The whole is in sober good taste, in keeping with the British Army. With the regimental badge of each on his headstone and flower arrangements that seem personalised there is a sense of intimacy. It is as if the soldier buried there has made that plot his own. In silent reflection here or there it seems one is by the grave of a dear one.

A harmony and balance of classical architecture

The way-in is noteworthy : a narrow entrance in the stone-work, having a small gate in ornamental ironwork. In all British Cemeteries there is an air of restraint. Not one contains a statue; the same style in plain limestone is found everywhere. The spirit and harmony of classical architecture blends in the lay-out of gardens in pleasing proportions where all is peace.

One monument is common to all : The Cross of Sacrifice designed by R. Bloomfield. It is a Latin Cross surmounting an octagonal plinth. A bronze sword on the vertical stonework, it is the sole dominant factor. The Stone of Remembrance designed by E. Luytas in the form of an altar, in the open air is found only in the larger cemeteries. It is engraved with the text from Ecclesiastes : "Their Name Liveth For Evermore." In the largest cemeteries there are visitors' halls. These consist of two pavilions, one each side of the main alley, built of limestone in classical style. In one of these is kept a register of graves and a visitors' book to sign and write impressions.

In the other pavilion is a map, to be found in all cemeteries illustrating the Battle of Normandy. A short notice gives the number of graves, the nationality of the soldiers and the operations in which they took part. In smaller cemeteries the elements mentioned may be confined to one pavilion only. There may be variations from one place to another but the same style is dominant. Occasionally architects make use of differing ground levels to make terraces around elements of masonry.

A feature, characteristic of British cemeteries of the Second World War are the pergolas to support climbing plants. These can be seen around the buildings or on either side of the alleys. Benches of wood or stone, typical of English parks allow visitors to rest in the course of their visit.

A touching book in stone

The Royal Charter of 1917 established a fundamental principle : individual commemoration. An identical headstone, rectangular, of Italian Limestone, honours each soldier without any apparent difference. In straight lines, they appear at first sight, like a military parade.

On approaching, the visitor discovers little by little all the individual features that form this army. On each one, finely engraved, are the Arms of his regiment. Under which is his Number, Rank, his Name and Unit. His religion is symbolised by a Latin Cross or a Star of David. The headstone sometimes leads one to believe that the combattant was agnostic. At the foot, half hidden by flowers is engraved an inscription chosen by his closest relative or friend.

From stone to stone the differences appear. A multitude of regimental emblems with figures and names that give rise to thoughts of the immense Army of the British Empire in origin from the English counties. An entire book of pictures, parades before the visitor's eyes, struck always by the youth of the soldiers. The grief of their closest is read from their 'adieux' that they have dedicated to their departed : "So dearly loved, every day in silence we remember".

Sometimes the spacing is broken to bring together the stones of those whose bodies could not be separated, often crews of the Royal Air Force. Other stones here and there have no name : just an inscription : "A soldier of the 1939-1945 War - Known unto God". A few squares further and the maple-leaf identifies a Canadian or a fern a New Zealander. Headstones differ somewhat for soldiers not belonging to the Commonwealth.

Just a garden with flowers

The horticultural aspect is described in a publication by the Commonwealth War Graves Commission : "The impression of a garden must be given, rather than that of an ordinary cemetery... A place where a harmony of elements combine to form a sense of tranquility in a peaceful setting". From the trimmed low hedge on the periphery to the flowers at the foot of the grave-stones, everything blends to give the impression of a garden where great trees spread over green lawns.

In some cases (Hermanville, Banneville-Sannerville), an expanse of green and foliage greets the visitor prior to entering the grave-yard. It is an English garden of high horticultural standard (a variety of flowers and colours in winter...) as if passing through a secluded spot to a private garden. Otherwise, it may be simply clumps of different shrubs that line a drive laid to lawn and impeccably kept. All the alleys are laid to lawn from the wide ones to the paths between the stones. The visitor may wander at will across the whole expanse.

There are a great deal of flowers as much from the shrubs as on the wistaria, honeysuckle and climbing roses that enfurl the pergolas. At the foot of the grave-stones runs a bed of flowers with here and there a few small shrubs, that gives the impression of individual gardens. Perenniels and rosebushes, Polyanthus burst with colour against the white of the stones. From early spring and through the summer they flower but are at their best in June.

THE CEMETERIES OF THE COMMONWEALTH

Like their British cousins

Canadian troops were engaged on all fronts in the Battle of Normandy, from the Landings to the last skirmish in the Falaise Gap. Numerous cemeteries marked the path of the Canadian Units from the sea to the Department of the Orne.

In 1945 the War Graves Commission regrouped the war-graves. The Canadians were re-interred on two sites, chosen among the provisional grave-yards which were possible to extend. At Reviers close to the sea are the soldiers who fell in the wake of the Landings and in the advance on Caen whilst those interred at Bretteville-sur-Laize were killed during the liberation of Caen or in taking the Falaise Pocket.

These cemeteries were laid-out by the British following the rules laid down in 1917 by the Imperial War Graves Commission.

Islands of foliage in the Fields

The two Canadian cemeteries lie in open country, islands of foliage in the middle of cultivated fields. Laid out on high ground they dominate the landscape and offer distant views. Although their appearance scarcely differs from British cemeteries they are easily identifiable. The isolation of the site and the rather severe-looking buildings impose at once a sense of awe and reflection. Within, the atmosphere is similar to that of British cemeteries, laid out in the same way to the same effect. There is the same likeness to a secluded garden with flower arrangements at the foot of each head-stone. The symbolic monuments found in British cemeteries are here too : The Cross of Sacrifice and the Stone of Remembrance.

The headstones are alike, made of white limestone, rectangular with a rounded top. The national emblem, a maple leaf is engraved at the head of each, except for the Royal Canadian Air Force and the Navy where the insignia of the Arm of Service appears instead. For other soldiers of the Commonwealth their headstones carry either their Regimental Badge or the Arms of their Country. A French visitor is surprised sometimes to read a name with a familiar ring ; it is the grave of a soldier from Quebec.

The inscription at the foot of the stone is not less touching. The maple leaf is everywhere, above on the flags flying in the wind, on the gates at Cintheaux, on the headstones and of course on the trees planted there.

THE CANADIAN CEMETERIES

Bretteville-sur-Laize Cintheaux   *Calvados*

In this cemetery are 2,958 graves of which 2,782 are Canadian, 80 British, 4 Australian, one New Zealander and one French.

Not far from Cintheaux, it is in the middle of ploughed fields. As with British cemeteries, only the neo-classical buildings and low walls are visible proclaiming this as a place on the landscape set apart.

There are several areas of transition : first, a narrow entrance in limestone gives on to wide lawns bounded at either end by unusual shell-shaped stone shelters. From here, through the colonnade of the entrance building, though still outside the cemetery proper can be seen the main memorials : the Stone of Remembrance and the Cross of Sacrifice and even the tops of the tomb stones.

The entrance proper consists of a double colonnade linking two pavilions that open inwards. In these are the register of graves and the visitors' book.

Site : 12 km south of Caen

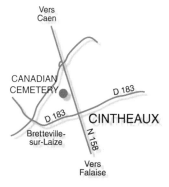

Next nearest war cemetery : Urville (Polish) 5 km.

Bény - Reviers   *Calvados*

There are 2,049 graves in this cemetery : 2,044 are Canadian, 4 British and one French. In 1944 provisional cemeteries were set up near the villages of Bény-sur-mer and Reviers; the present site was chosen for its position on rising ground and view of the sea.

On the road-side is a double entrance flanked by pillars set in a wall of white limestone, then from stone to vegetation where Maples open out on to a large lawn. The symetry is impeccable. The rows of Maples are faultlessly aligned with the twin pavilions in which the register of graves and the visitors' book are kept. At that level one can take in the cemetery, the surrounding country and the sea beyond.

Two small square towers are linked by flagstones. Steps in the centre lead up to the Stone of Remembrance. In front of this is a space bounded by low, trimmed hedges where stand four stone benches, on which to meditate or rest.

Site : 3 km south of Courseulles 15 km north of Caen

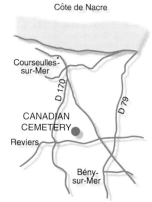

Next nearest war cemetery : Douvres-la-Délivrande (British) 6 km.

Men and their stories

Noble adolescents…

In April 1943, Gérard DORÉ joined up. He was 15 years 9 months old.

He dreamt perhaps of heroic fights that fashion heroes. He landed at Courseulles-sur-mer on 8th July 1944 and took part in operations south of Caen. He was cut down by enemy machine-gun fire. He was sixteen.

Three comrades older than he was are buried at his side, their dreams unfinished, their youth intact. 147 others were less than twenty.

Gérard DORÉ lies in the cemetery at Cintheaux. With 2,959 graves it is the biggest Canadian War Cemetery of the Second World War.

Homage rendered to the courage of Canadian Youth and to Gérard DORÉ on the Anniversary of his death in July 1998.

Faithful brothers…

In the little village of Billy a few kilometres away from the cemetery at Cintheaux, the people remember this pilot of 26, shot down by German Ack-ack, in the Falaise Pocket. A plaque near the "Mairie" is in honour of Jimmy LANFRANCHI, who died on the field of honour on 28th June 1944.

His two younger brothers have visited the grave for the past 35 years. In 1999 after 5 years of research, the Curator of the "Musée Memorial de la Bataille de Normandie" in Bayeux, Jean-Pierre BÉNAMOU, came to the conclusion that Jimmy LANFRANCHI was not buried at Cintheaux ; it was another Canadian named Lorne CURRY. When Jimmy died, his two brothers in their grief, learned that his plane had been shot down at Proussy, 30 kilometres away. A plaque has now been placed at Proussy, since this is the place concerned. Walter and Louis realise this. Both have obtained authorisation to be buried alongside their brother.

An act of Remembrance in the Cemetery at Cintheaux.

THE CEMETERIES OF THE COMMONWEALTH

Visits by one or more members of the family

After the First World War the Imperial War Graves Commission was created by Royal Charter, taking over 'Army Graves Registration and Enquiries', for the setting up of cemeteries world-wide, wherever soldiers of the British Empire had fallen. Today the Commonwealth War Graves Commission takes its place. It is a private organization, the budget of which depends on grants and subsidies from the associated governments : United Kingdom, Canada, New Zealand, South Africa and Australia.

The Commission looks after 2,400 sites world-wide and deals with research for missing soldiers. The personnel consists of gardeners who are Commonwealth expatriates or, more often men recruited and trained on the spot. Each team has a head-gardner who, in turn is responsible to the Director of Horticulture. Only a few cemeteries, like Bayeux have their own staff. Other cemeteries are maintained by visiting personnel.

The number of visitors varies from one cemetery to another according to its position : near a town or a main road. Their size determines the likelihood that they will be visited singly or by a family rather than by coaches of tourists. The attitude of visitors to British cemeteries is quite different to that of other cemeteries. Soon after their arrival groups of visitors split up and wander at will, between the rows of grave-stones, halting here and there as an inscription, an epitaph or flowers catches the eye. It is in the small cemeteries off the beaten track of tourists that emotions are strongest.

These places in the middle of nowhere suggest somehow that relatives may arrive at any moment and pause in reflection by the grave of one of theirs. A very deep sense of calm pervades. Peace is ever present in these restful spots, the silence unbroken except by the songs of birds.

THE BRITISH CEMETERIES

Banneville - Sannerville   *Calvados*

Municipality of Banneville
2,175 graves : 2,150 British, 11 Canadian, 5 Australian, 2 New Zealander, 5 Polish, 2 unknown

Situated outside the village, near the R.N. 175 the cemetery lies on the edge of a small wood. Once through the small gate the scent of flowers twists and turns between the two beds leading to the Grave-stones. A tiny chapel, the only building, houses the registers and the account of the Battle of Normandy. Pergolas support climbing Hydrangers, Honeysuckle and Wistaria.

Most of the soldiers buried at Banneville were killed in the second week of July following the liberation of Caen and in the course of Operation GOODWOOD. Men who fell in action that followed, culminating in the closure of the Falaise Gap and the German withdrawal during the last week of August 1944, are also buried here.

Site : 7 km south-west of Caen, 3 km west of Troarn

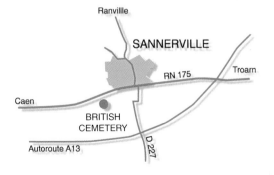

Next nearest war cemetery : Ranville (British) 7 km.

Bayeux   *Calvados*

4,648 graves : 3,935 British, 17 Australian, 181 Canadians, 8 New Zealander, 1 South African, 25 Polish, 3 French, 2 Czech, 2 Italian, 7 Russian, 466 German, 1 unknown

Bayeux was liberated the day after the Landings on 7th June 1944. The first cemetery was laid out near a Field Hospital. Soldiers who died in other hospitals in the area were buried there subsequently. Bayeux is the largest British Cemetery in France from the Second World War and the most cosmopolitan with 11 nationalities.

The layout of the cemetery is in perfect symmetry. Beyond an entrance hall, stand two small towers, one either side of the Stone of Remembrance. Among the graves of the Commonwealth there are also different types of headstones for the Polish, French, Czech, Italian and Russian soldiers, as well as a sizeable German section. The cemetery is bounded by a low hedge of trimmed Beech leaving a view of the Cathedral and the City. On the other side of the road stands the Memorial with the names inscribed of 1,537 British, 270 Canadians and 1 South African. These are the names of soldiers. Sailors and Airmen are commemorated on their own memorials in Britain.

Site : Western side of the Boulevard, (By-pass) near the War Museum

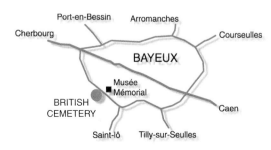

Next nearest war cemetery : Ryes (British) 10 km.

Brouay   *Calvados*

377 graves : 375 British, 2 Canadian

Situated on what was the Front Line from 10th to 18th June 1944, the village of Brouay was the junction of British and Canadian troops. The soldiers buried here fell in the fight to encircle Caen to the south.

Situated near the village church, the cemetery is laid out on a gentle slope adjacent to the churchyard that gives access to it. A low stone wall separates and sustains the level of each. The visitors' hall, roofed in slate, marks the entrance from which is seen, on a clearing of lawn, the Cross of Sacrifice. The head-stones, unaligned are mainly to the left of the entrance.

This little cemetery, planted with apple-trees has a great deal of charm with views of the church and churchyard, neighbouring houses and surrounding countryside.

Site : between Caen and Bayeux 1.5 km south of R.N. 13

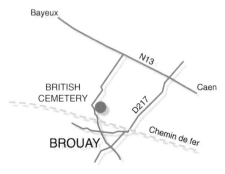

Next nearest war cemetery : Secqueville-en-Bessin (British) 4 km.

Cambes-en-Plaine   *Calvados*

224 British graves

Most of the soldiers buried here are from the North Staffordshire and South Staffordshire Regiments which played an active part in the battle to liberate Caen on 8th and 9th July 1944. The cemetery of Cambes-en-Plaine is situated in the former park of the Château : bitterly disputed territory in the summer of 1944.

On the edge of the village near a new housing development this little cemetery is hidden under poplars. It is bounded by hedge-rows with a variety of species of flowering shrubs. Views on to the adjoining formal park give to this little enclave an impression of added space. The rounded entrance has a flat roof and houses the visitors' hall. The Cross of Sacrifice couched in the shade of tall trees faces a single square of headstones.

In a setting of some excellence, this little cemetery adds purpose to a walk or outing with a sense of peace and rest in one of the rare islets of foliage on the plain of tillage, north of Caen.

Site : 6 km north of Caen

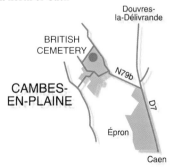

Next nearest war cemetery :
Douvres-la-Délivrande (British) 8 km.

THE BRITISH CEMETERIES

Chouain - Jérusalem *Calvados*

47 graves : 46 British, 1 Czech

The soldiers buried at Chouain had fought from the first day of the battle at Tilly-sur-Seulles on 8th June 1944. Killed at Douet de Chouain 35 soldiers were interred in a field near the hamlet of Jérusalem. Less than a mile away a Field Hospital was set up near Belval Farm and about ten soldiers were buried nearby.

After the War, at the request of the Mayor the authorities kept the graves there. The municipality gave the ground near Belval Farm and those buried at the hamlet of Jérusalem were transferred there. The cemetery took the name of Chouain-Jérusalem.

It is the smallest British War Cemetery in France. The entrance on the Tilly-Bayeux road is through a small gateway of wrought-iron flanked by two stone pillars. Some garden flagstones set between the bushes and conifers lead to the graves aligned concentrically in three rows, facing the Cross of Sacrifice. A stock-fence and hedge separates the cemetery from the farm of which it seems a part.

Site : Between Bayeux and Tilly-sur-Seulles 8 km S.E. of Bayeux

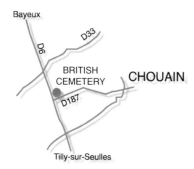

Next nearest war cemetery : Tilly-sur-Seulles (British) 7 km.

Douvres-la-Délivrande *Calvados*

1,123 graves : 927 British, 11 Canadian, 3 Australian, 1 Polish, 180 German, 1 unknown

Three kilometres from the Landing Beach JUNO the German radar station on the Basly road at Douvres became for several days an entrenched camp. An RAMC operating theatre was set up in a convent at La Délivrande. The first casualties buried here were killed on 6th July. Later, soldiers killed between Caen and the coast were also interred. The cemetery entrance on the outskirts of the town is easy to find on the Caen road. A square pavilion with a pointed top, roofed in stone is flanked by pergolas. Visible through the opening in the pavilion, the Cross of Sacrifice stands at the end of the central alley. On a small mound of turf it is bounded by low walls. The grave-stones are set out symmetrically on either side of the central alley bordered with clipped yew trees. The German section is on the right. The stones are of a different type and shape. Oddly enough the one Polish soldier has been buried apart from the others.

Site : 11 km north of Caen

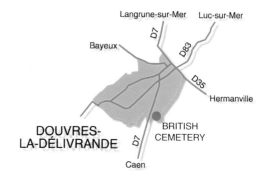

Next nearest war cemeteries : Hermanville (British) 7 km - Cambes-en-Plaine (British) 8 km.

Fontenay-le-Pesnel *Calvados*

520 graves : 457 British, 4 Canadian, 59 German

In the cemetery at Fontenay-le-Pesnel are buried the soldiers involved in clashes west of Caen in June and July 1944, notably those who took part in Operation EPSOM on 26th June. The units involved were mainly drawn from : Hallamshire, East Lancashire, Royal Warwickshire and the Durham Light Infantry Regiments.

Arriving on the Route Departementale 139 facing the road to the cemetery, stands a Memorial. This monument in limestone is surmounted by a cross; on it are engraved transversally the arms of the British Regiments whose men lie at Fontenay-le-Pesnel.

The cemetery is in the middle of a field on the edge of a little wood, some 300 metres from the Memorial. First in view are the white roofs of the visitors' halls and the Cross of Sacrifice emerging from the fields.
The arrangement within is unusual ; the graves in three sections on the left are set out in the form of a fan.

Site : 12 km west of Caen, on the road to Caumont l'Éventé

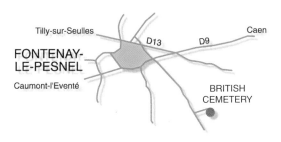

Next nearest war cemeteries : Tilly-sur-Seulles (British) 5 km - SAINT-MANVIEU (British) 5 km.

Hermanville *Calvados*

1,005 graves : 986 British, 13 Canadian, 3 Australian, 3 French

Close to the sea and to Landing Beach SWORD, Hermanville was taken early in the day on 6th June 1944 by men of the 1st Battalion of the South Lancashire Regiment. They were joined later in the day by the Shropshire Light Infantry supported by the armour of the Staffordshire Yeomanry. Most of the soldiers buried here, fell on 6th June or in the first exchanges in the advance on Caen.

Not far from the village church, the cemetery stands alone at the end of a lane bordering a wood. Through a little gate a flagstone path winds between the trees and rockeries with roses and heather. In January there is an immaculate carpet of snowdrops. At the far end, only the Cross of Sacrifice stands out. The whole gives an impression of a well-kept little public square that fades only as the head stones come in sight : modest graves in the shade of apple-trees. The visitors' hall of rough-hewn limestone under a slate roof is reminiscent of little chapels in the region. Its main façade has three open bays consisting of gothic arches.

Site : 13 km north of Caen

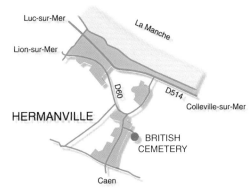

Next nearest war cemetery : Douvres-la-Délivrande (British) 7 km.

THE BRITISH CEMETERIES

Hottot-les-Bagues   *Calvados*

1,137 graves : 965 British, 34 Canadian, 3 Australian, 2 New Zealanders, 1 South African, 132 German.

The soldiers who lie in this cemetery were killed in the action to encircle Caen to the south, notably in clashes near Tilly-sur-Seulles. Most of those buried here came from provisional cemeteries nearby, set up during the battle.

Along Route Départementale N° 9, the usual front hedge has been replaced by a bank, planted with large Oaks and bushes of Box. The cemetery is laid-out very symmetrically, terracing the sloping ground to three levels. The entrance is aligned with the central alley, the Cross of Sacrifice and at the far end the visitors' hall, the façade of which is open through three arcades and flanked by two pergolas. A split-level in the centre creates two distinct sections with a bank laid to lawn, between them. The Cross, surmounting steps, stands at the centre. In open country, the cemetery is restrained and peaceful, with unrestricted views over surrounding fields and foliage.

Site : 20 km west of Caen

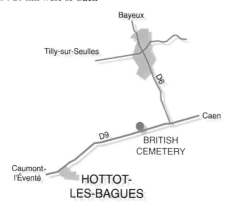

Next nearest war cemetery : Tilly-sur-Seulles (British) 3 km.

Ranville   *Calvados*

2,562 graves : 2,151 British, 76 Canadian, 1 Australian, 1 Belgian, 322 German, 2 unknown

Near the site of the historic Pegasus Bridge, Ranville was the first village in France to be liberated. During the night of 5th June 1944, the British 6th Airborne Division parachuted on to the banks of the Orne to seize the two bridges. The first casualties were buried in the churchyard and then outside its walls. Soldiers who fell in the action to liberate Caen were interred on ground contiguous to th Ranville churchyard.

The war cemetery is an integral part of the village. The entrance, opposite an old mill, has a stone porch, surrounded by low stone-walls. On either side is a low trimmed hedge of Beech. Inside this a line of young oaks provide a screen from the road. The first impression is curious : on either side of a narrow alley the headstones are unaligned : a striking departure from the usual order of things. Between the stones are roses : red, yellow and rose-coloured with tufts of Lavender.

Site : 11 km NE of Caen, 2 km from Pegasus Bridge

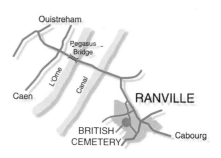

Next nearest war cemetery : Banneville (British) 7 km.

Ryes - Bazenville *Calvados*

979 graves : 630 British, 21 Canadian, 1 Australian, 1 Polish, 326 German

The village of Ryes is situated a few kilometres from the Landing Beaches in the GOLD sector and the artificial port of Arromanches where the men of 50th British Division landed on 6th June 1944. The cemetery at Bazenville was set up two days after the Landings.

Laid out on a plot below road-level from which it is bounded by a hedge-row of box and distanced by an area of lawn, the cemetery is in full view. The entrance on the road side is flanked by a trimmed hedge of Beech, in the centre of which is a double entrance in a low stone wall. On each side of the Cross of Sacrifice, are pergolas entwined with Wistaria, Honeysuckle, Roses and Virginia-creeper. Magnificent clumps of Lavender border the alley, which runs crosswise, leading to two small visitors' halls. The head-stones are arranged symmetrically on either side of the alleys. The German graves at the far end, are detached from the rest.

Site : 8 km east of Bayeux, 6 km south of Arromanches

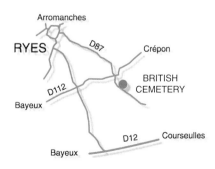

Next nearest war cemetery : Bayeux (British) 10 km.

Saint-Charles-de-Percy *Calvados*

789 graves : 786 British, 3 Canadian

In this vicinity the Front advanced slowly between Caumont-l'Éventé, liberated on 13th June 1944 and Vire and Villers-Bocage not taken until the first week of August. Those who were laid to rest at Saint-Charles-de-Percy were killed following the break-out of British troops to Vire at the end of July and the beginning of August 1944. Other soldiers who fell in the surrounding Normandy countryside are also to be found here.

Right in the heart of the Bocage this isolated little cemetery is located only by its entrance porch. Around it are rough hedgerows where wild-cherry predominate, forming a tight enclave. On either side of the colonnaded entrance porch is a tiny flat-roofed visitors' room. At the end of a wide alley stands the Cross of Sacrifice with ample space on each side. At the foot of each gravestone perennials flower throughout the summer months.

Site : 12 km NE of Vire, 20 km south of Villers-Bocage

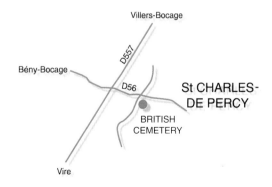

Next nearest war cemetery : Marigny (German) 60 km.

Saint-Désir-de-Lisieux   *Calvados*

598 graves : 569 British, 16 Canadian, 6 Australian, 1 New Zealander, 5 South African, 1 American

The entrance is side-ways on and opens on to large lawns. The Cross of Sacrifice is aligned with the central alley. Beyond is a small octogonal kiosk, the only visitors' room. Over a low trimmed-hedge on three sides are views of the surrounding fields, distant countryside and the neighbouring German cemetery. Inside the hedgerow bordering the road are trees and flowering shrubs. Facing the Cross, apple-trees line the central alley and clumps of Lavender mark each row of headstones. From Spring time to Summer, perrennial plants and rose-trees in flower give each tomb a burst of colour.

The site was first used by the Germans in the Battle of Normandy. Later, the British buried their dead here by the side of the German cemetery. These soldiers lost their lives during the German retreat to the Seine. A few soldiers of the First World War have been transferred here.
In spite of its proximity to the road, the R.N. 13, this little cemetery in the heart of the Pays d'Auge is a pleasant place to wander into on fine days.

Site : 4 km west of Lisieux near the R.N. 13

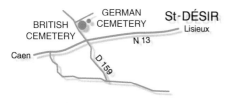

Next nearest war cemetery : Saint-Désir-de-Lisieux (German) a few hundred yards along the road.

Saint-Manvieu - Norrey   *Calvados*

2,183 graves : 1,623 British, 3 Canadian, 1 Australian, 556 Germans

From mid-June 1944 until the liberation of Caen on 9th July, clashes were numerous in this sector : the Battle for Tilly, operations EPSOM and JUPITER and the taking of the aerodrome at Carpiquet on 6th July. British and Canadian Troops sustained large losses in these assaults.

From the Route Départementale a path laid to lawn leads up to the cemetery entrance. The borders with numerous species of flowering plants : Asters, Cotoneasters, Potentilla, Meadowsweet, clumps of Heather and Lavender Escallonia and Vegelia, provide a great variety of flowers and scents. The entrance between two pillars opens on to the lower corner of the cemetery. It is divided right across into sixteen squares of graves, each row is marked by a clump of purple Berberis. Amongst the perennials, yellow roses are predominant in the first section whilst in the second most are pink. German graves, which are more numerous than in other cemeteries have been placed at each end. There are big trees on the periphery : Horse chestnuts, Silver birch, Yoke-elms, Sweet chestnuts and a magnificent Catalpa.

Site : 11 km west of Caen

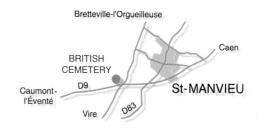

Next nearest war cemetery : Fontenay-le-Pesnel (British) 5 km.

Secqueville-en-Bessin *Calvados*

117 graves : 98 British, 18 Germans, 1 Allied soldier unknown

Secqueville-en-Bessin was a junction between British and Canadian troops. Soldiers who lie here were killed in the fighting in the advance on Caen. The cemetery began near a Field Operating Theatre. Larger than it now is, Canadians buried here were transferred to Reviers.

This is one of the smallest British cemeteries in the district. It lies outside the village, amid fields at the end of a cul-de-sac. The first one sees of it is the Cross of Sacrifice between two Yew trees, rising from surrounding field crops. The cemetery, bounded by a clipped hedge is L-shaped. In the long section are the British with the Cross of Sacrifice at the centre whilst the Germans lie in the shorter piece.

Though modest in size and isolated the cemetery leaves a strong impression : the soldiers who fell in the fighting, died here, otherwise they would not be buried in such isolated countryside.

Site : mid-way between Caen and Bayeux slightly north of the R.N. 13

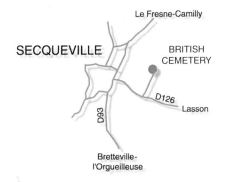

Next nearest war cemetery : Reviers (Canadian) 11 km.

Tilly-sur-Seulles *Calvados*

1,222 graves : 986 British, 2 New Zealanders, 1 Canadian, 1 Australian, 232 Germans

Shortly after the Landings, fighting took place around Tilly-sur-Seulles. Mainly 49th, 50th and 7th Armoured Divisions (British) were involved. Tilly was not liberated until 18th June, following violent clashes which were to continue until mid-July 1944.

The cemetery lies near the road in open country behind a hedge of trimmed Beech not far from the centre of Tilly.

Across the entire width on either side of the Cross, stand two porches flanked by 'jardinières' with creeping coniferous shrubs. Beyond are pergolas, their pillars entwined with Wistaria, Honeysuckle, Clematis, and Virginia-creeper. At each end is a semi-circular stone bench surrounded by a close-clipped hedge. At the foot of the headstones numbers of red yellow and pink Roses are mixed with the perennials.

Site : 12 km S.E. of Bayeux, 20 km west of Caen

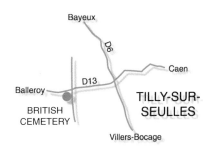

Next nearest war cemetery : Hottot-les-Bagues (British) 3 km.

The Americans, the French, then the Volksbund

In the course of the Second World War about 250,000 Germans were killed on French soil. During the Battle of Normandy, with limited time at their disposal, German troops were forced to abandon their dead or bury them summarily where they fell. On occasion they were able to give them more dignified graves after regrouping the fallen. Behind the lines the Allies continued the task of burying the Dead of both sides.

When the War ended, German cemeteries were put in the hands of the French Authorities. Isolated graves and small cemeteries were spread over 1,400 municipalities in Lower Normandy. Under the Treaty of Versailles, France had the task of verifying and looking after German graves on her territory. The feeling of rancour towards the former Occupant, still ever present, the existence of this mass of graves dispersed across the Bocage of Normandy was not well accepted by the population. The 'Service Français des Sépultures' proceeded to transfer them to the larger provisional cemeteries, set up after the Battle, at La Cambe, le Chêne-Guérin, Marigny, Orglandes, and Saint-Désir-de-Lisieux. At the end of the Forties, the graves from the little cemeteries were taken up. In spite of the requests of families, Germany enfeebled after the War, was unable to repatriate the bodies of her soldiers. The Volksbund, an association of German people for the care of war-graves took over the work under the direction of its Architect-in-Chief, Robert Tischler. From 1948 onwards he put in hand, plans for the lay-out of new cemeteries.

Whilst awaiting a peace treaty several international agreements between 1952 and 1966 progressively transferred the responsibilty for the lay-out, exhuming and regrouping of the German Dead to the German Federal Republic. The Bilateral Accord of 1954 provided for the permanent cemeteries of Champigny-St-André, (in the Eure), La Cambe, Marigny and Orglandes originally set up by American troops, Saint-Désir-de-Lisieux, set up by the German Army and Mont-d'Huisnes opened later. Meanwhile, the Germans could return to these sites and the Volksbund was made responsible by the German Authorities to execute the tasks resulting from these different accords. In 1956 began the lengthy task of identifying the victims and the regrouping in permanent cemeteries of those taken from an area extending from the east to the south of Normandy. Thus the 1,600 graves at Le-Chêne-Guérin were transferred to the nearest German cemeteries. The number of graves at Marigny after the Americans had transferred theirs to Colleville was 4,246. It was increased to 5,713 by the transfer of German graves by the French. Today there are 11,169.

In 1957, the Volksbund began work on the lay-out and extension of cemeteries. For this they used the services of independent architects who in turn used gardeners landscape specialists and artists for the design and construction of their cemeteries. Youth Camps took on a large part of the digging and arrangement. At La Cambe, they took part in the erection of the 'Tumulus' : a burial mound of 296 combattants. Work continued until 20th and 21st September 1961, dates of the formal inaugurations of German military cemeteries in Lower Normandy.

Created later, the necropolis at Mont-d'Huisnes was a work of a different conception. This great funeral monument was designed by Johannes Krahn in 1959, a Frankfort architect. It contains the remains of a large number of soldiers exhumed in 1961 by the Volksbund, from Departements nearby as well as Morbihan, Loir-et-Cher, Vienne and from the Channel Islands. It was inaugurated on 14th September 1963. Today 11,956 Germans repose there.

Some British cemeteries continue to look after graves of German soldiers whose bodies have never been exhumed by the Volksbund. At Saint-Manvieu and Ranville, for example, there are 556 and 322 German graves respectively to be counted alongside 1,627 and 2,240 Allied graves, as witness to the fierce fighting in these sectors on the day following the Landings.

Today over 70,000 German soldiers are interred in the Military cemeteries of Normandy, of which there are 3,735 at Saint-Désir and 10,152 at Orglandes. The 21,222 graves at La Cambe make it the largest of all. Every year Germans are to be found at the graves of those who fell, on the soil of Normandy.

THE GERMAN CEMETERIES

Gravity and Grandeur

On penetrating a German cemetery the visitor is struck first by the gravity and grandeur that emanates from it. All seems designed to contribute to this : the arrangement of the entrance, the sombre choice of materials, severity and size, the exactitude of workmanship, even the majestic bearing of the trees that dominate the whole. The atmosphere is one of meditation. All reference to the events of war is blotted out. The symbolism goes back to Scandinavian mythology. Here is the entrance to "Walhalla", a paradise reserved for warriors who died as heroes. At the outset, in cemeteries for the vanquished, dignified space seemed appropriate, without flowers, sober without artifice, where a desire to be genuine is greatly apparent.

The outside of the cemeteries can be seen from within but not the inside from without. The wooded banks of hedgerows on their boundaries qualify as ramparts and have been kept or reconstituted, so that the cemetery melts into the surrounding countryside. Often remote from roads or habitation, a gatehouse on the end of a wall is the only sign of a cemetery's presence. It constitutes a kind of geographical and meditative space through which to pass prior to penetrating the land of the departed. At first, an entrance porch, dark and narrow in which the view is halved and against the light. The effect is striking. It may be the sight of something symbolic : the Tumulus at La Cambe or the Cross at Huisnes or some other focal point.

The visitor wanders at will, on a lawn under great trees, the breaks in which, light the way to the centre to form a vast clearing. The shade and volume of the place, given by the trees is in extent, broken only by the lines of head-stones, as at La Cambe and Orglandes, or the beds of perennials and groups of crosses as at Saint-Désir and Marigny. The grey of the occasional paved alley, the dark, low crosses, the imposing monuments, the regular spacing the absence of distinctive signs, all contribute strange emotions.

At Huisnes-sur-Mer, the impression is quite different. Only the approaches and the entrance are landscaped, disguising the cemetery itself. Inside is a building circular in shape and open to the sky. The interior is laid to lawn, under which lie the Fallen. Within this enclosure only the roses serve to lighten the gravity and austerity of this place.

Surrounded by Tall Hedgerows

In concern for discretion the desire at the outset, to blend the cemetery into surrounding country was done by heightening the banks of hedgerows to form a dense enclosure. To form an inner line, further bushes have been added later. More recently ornamental shrubs have been added and carpeting plants, to form a low and varied broken hedge. Amongst the varied species planted are Viburnum, Rhododendron, Buddleia, Mountain Ash and Holly. At Orglandes the original 'bocage' hedgerows are preserved with care to keep the enclosure as it was.

There are no individual plantings on the graves, the only touch of colour comes from flouring shrubs on the periphery near the entrance. At La Cambe however the Tumulus is bounded by a rockery of red roses. At Saint-Désir there are Irises planted in beds at the foot of the crosses which in spring colour the lawn from end to end in violet. At Marigny wide beds of St John's Wort mark out in yellow the alleys parallel to the lines of graves.

Grey granite and red sandstone

There a few characteristics, common to the constructions and lay-out of the Lower Normandy cemeteries. There is a strong stamp of Germanic art and architecture from which all military implications are absent. The entrance both at Marigny and Orglandes is built in the form of a chapel. The proportions of the former are those of small churches in the region. The latter is more imposing, built of local stone, square in form, it has a German tower. In the two Calvados cemeteries is a massive building with the flat roof, rectangular in shape : in granite at La Cambe and in red sandstone with a colonnade at Saint-Désir.

Through a monumental metal gate or a very decorative grill one gains access to a sombre hall. From here, beneath either a plain lintel or an arch, a massive though narrow door opens directly on to the grave-yard. Either side of the hall-way are rooms with a register of graves and a visitors' book. On the wall, under the emblem of the Volksbund is inscribed : *"Hier ruhen deutsche Soldaten"*, Here repose German Soldiers. To mark the sacred character of the place, in a niche at Marigny, there is a mosaic of the Virgin with the dead Christ across her knees and at Orglandes of Christ giving blessing.

The alleys are rarely paved. At La Cambe the one leading from the entrance to the Tumulus is paved with granite flag-stones. A father and mother watching over their children stand on either side of a great Maltese Cross : these are sculptured in basalt brought from Germany and dominate the summit of the Tumulus.

Not relative to the number of graves Maltese Crosses aligned in threes at Marigny and in fives at La Cambe are the only vertical elements that break the surface of the lawns. Carved in basalt, these dark and rugged crosses are short and thick.

Discreet grave-stones placed among the greenery

In the form of a Teutonic Cross, square with short branches, German headstones may be upright as at Saint-Désir or Orglandes. They are cut from red sandstone at Saint-Désir or in light grey stone at Orglandes. They may also be placed horizontally in the turf of the lawn as at La Cambe and Marigny. There they are discreet ceramic plaques.

The alignment of the stones depends on the cemetery lay-out. If vertical they carry two, sometimes three names. They are between two rows of graves. When placed in the turf, they can be read from one side or the other of the alley that marks out and separates the graves. Each usually carries only two names. When known, the inscriptions mention the surname, name, rank and dates of birth and death. Otherwise the inscritpion reads : "Ein Deutscher Soldat". There is no reference to an army or a command. These are soldiers without an army who lie here.

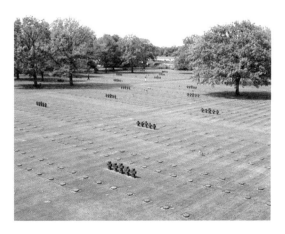

THE GERMAN CEMETERIES
"Reconciliation over the tombs, working for Peace."

The Volksbund Deutsche Kriegsgräberfürsorge, a people's association for the care of German war graves was founded in December 1919. It deals with the care of all German war cemeteries abroad, on behalf of the German Government and fulfils other missions in the sphere of human rights. It is widely supported by the people of Germany whose moral and financial support is indispensable and completes government aid.

The work of the Volksbund personnel is assisted by numbers of voluntary helpers. Under the direction of a National Bureau and a Regional Superintendant based at Marigny, the guardians have charge of one or more cemeteries. The gardeners are trained on site and work in teams, moving from one cemetery to another. Regular appeals for help are made to Youth Camps.

It is difficult to give figures but several hundred thousand visitors come to the German War Cemeteries in Normandy every year. Being on the circuit of the Landings and accessible from the main road La Cambe is the most frequented. Marigny, Saint-Désir and Orglandes, away from tourist itineraries, get only a few visitors daily.

A few wreaths and bouquets placed discreetly at the foot of grave-stones mark the passage of a parent or close relative or friend. Most visitors are not Germans. Most visits are brief and are beyond political considerations. Remarks in the visitors' Book, all nations included, largely echo the message of Peace, of the Volksbund clearly stated by its motto : "Reconciliation above the tombs, working for Peace."

La Cambe   *Calvados*

21,222 German graves

The cemetery at La Cambe was set up by American troops who had a Field Hospital at La Cambe after taking the German Batteries and the Battle of Isigny. Since 1956 the work of the Volksbund has brought the number of graves to over 20,000 making La Cambe the largest war cemetery in the region.

The cemetery is over seventeen and a half acres in extent and is bounded by a 'bocage' type hedge-row with views over the marshes. Great trees, mainly Oak and Beech shade the lawns around a vast clearing. At the point where the two alleys cross is a tumulus six metres high, surmounted by a large cross of basalt between two statues. Groups of crosses and head-stones extend across the whole ; paths on the turf are around these memorials. The rectangular building, the wall between the cemetery and the car-park and the alley of flag-stones leading to the Tumulus are the only elements in stone and they are in grey granite. The over-all effect is one of majesty ; it is impressive and meditative.

Site : R.N. 13, 18 km west of Bayeux
1 km from the township

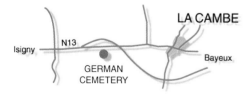

Next nearest war cemetery : Colleville-sur-Mer
(American) 12 km.

The last letter

Corporal Manfred KOLB, aged twenty, wrote home regularly. He did so on 11th June when his company moved to support the Front at Cherbourg. This was his last letter sent to his parents and sisters. Two days later, near Carentan he was mortally wounded by a bullet. He was buried in the cemetery at Bonneville with some of his comrades.

On 23rd June his family was informed of his death and received some of his personal effects. In 1945, this soldier killed at the Front was transferred by the American War Graves Service to the Orglandes War Cemetery. Unfortunately his documents were misplaced; his parents did not know where he was buried. In 1962 the Volksbund succeeded in locating the grave at Orglandes : Block 22, Row 8, Grave 291.

"Western Front, 12/06/44

My dears,

As the mail leaves today, I wanted to write to you straightaway so that I can give my letter to the despatch-rider. Starting with the most important : I am well and hope to continue to be. For three days we have been fighting on a bridge-head of American Landings and hope to give these big brothers a sound thrashing and send them home.

How are you all ? Are there still as many (air-raid) alerts ? I hope not. Did you get my last letter ? How are our kind relatives at Haslach, Hall, and Stuttgart ? Excuse my bad writing. I am in a trench only 60 cm wide that I dug with an American spade. On the other hand, I am sitting on something soft, silk and very good quality, a parachute and it is American too. I am finishing my letter slowly, trusting that I shall have the chance to write again in three days time before the next mail goes. I hope all this lot will be over soon, as I should like to be able to tell you lots of things in peace and quiet when I am home. My best wishes to you all and hope to see you soon.

Manfred"

He will never see his little girl

Valentin LEHRMANN was born on 27th September 1909 at Gelsenkirchen. His mother died when he was only two years old and he was brought up until his father remarried by his two elder sisters and his grand-parents.

Valentin decided to learn a trade and in 1934 passed his exam as a baker. Three months later he married his fiancée, Ellen Otto whom he had met at the Christian Youth Group ; he opened a bakery in the same year. All seemed set, therefore for a happy existence with every promise of success.

In 1939 the LEHRMANNS had their first daughter, Edith but a year later, war loomed menacingly over the family's good fortune. In 1940 Valentin was mobilised in the Wehrmacht ; in October his second child was born, a boy. His third child, a daughter saw the light of day on 26th May 1944.

Valentin, who was in France at the time, received news of the birth by telegram. But he was never to see his little girl.

On 6th June, the day of the Allied Landings, Full Corporal Valentin LEHRMANN was wounded and died next day. In 1946 a comrade-in-arms brought back to his widow, the personal effects found on Valentin LEHRMANN the day he died : his wedding-ring, Army-book, letters and a bible.

Valentin LEHRMANN lay first at Saint-Laurent-sur-Mer and was transferred later to the German War Cemetery at La Cambe : Block 2, Row 4, Grave 64.

Marigny *Manche*

Municipality of La-Chapelle-en-Juger
11,169 German graves

Sited in open country access to the Marigny cemetery is approached along a narrow winding road. It was set up by the Americans during the "War in the Hedges" and the battle for Saint-Lô. Following on from the Americans, then the French, the Volksbund transferred there, those from isolated graves and from many small cemeteries. The exhuming and the lay-out, took place from 1956 to 1961. At Marigny also is the Office of the person responsible for the Western Sector of the Volksbund which covers North West France.

Built of Schist, a stone quarried locally the entrance building is in the form of a church of the type found in the region. A small paved courtyard separates the tower from the nave, is followed by a somber part that gives access to the grave-yard itself. Over twelve acres, the cemetery is a square, divided into five long sections with beds of St John's Wort marking the alleys, divided by the alleys cross-wise, graves are marked by Maltese Crosses. These are grave-stones in ceramic, laid flat, inscribed with two or even three names. The St John's Wort with its yellow flowers and softened contours gives to Marigny quite a different character than the other German cemeteries.

Site : 12 km west of Saint-Lô

Next nearest war cemetery : Bayeux (British) 48 km.

THE GERMAN CEMETERIES

Orglandes *Manche*

10,152 German graves

Originally, Orglandes was a provisional cemetery, set up by the Americans after the advance on Cherbourg from Sainte-Mère-Église and Utah-Beach. It is just outside the Village along the D.24 road to Valognes. As with other German cemeteries the work of exhuming and the lay-out was done by the Volksbund between 1956 and 1961.

A square building surmounted by an impressive tower forms the cemetery entrance. The wall built on, gives the impression of an enclosed space. Quite the contrary, the slope and undulating ground has been kept, giving distant views of the surrounding countryside. The original banks and 'bocage' hedge-rows are maintained and these divide the twelve acres into four parcels. Much and varied foliage has been added which with the not too severe alignement of grey crosses lends a sense of both grandeur and simplicity to a site that is in perfect tune with the countryside.

Site : 10 km south of Valognes.

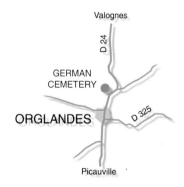

Next nearest war cemetery : Marigny (German) 50 km.

The Ossuaire at Mont-d'Huisnes *Manche*

Municipality of Huisnes-sur-Mer
11,956 German soldiers

Mont-d'Huisnes is the only German Mausoleum in France. It is laid-out on a hill, thirty metres high; 11,956 German War-dead are buried there. They were transferred there in 1961 by the Volksbund Service that exhumed them.

This is quite a different necropolis, from which, are wide views of Mont-Saint-Michel and the reclaimed land. The desire to keep the rural quality of the site has rendered it almost invisible. Mont-d'Huisnes has been kept as a natural hillock into which the necropolis has been hidden. Stone steps lead to the visitors' hall that opens on to a large plan with pins showing the Departements from which the Dead have been transferred. The Ossuary is built in the form of a cylinder on two levels around a courtyard laid to lawn and open to the sky. A great cross stands in the centre. On the outside a covered gallery has been built : at each level sixty-eight vaults in each of which repose a hundred and eighty bodies. At the opposite end to the entrance steps lead down to a landscaped terrace where, or from a belvedere one can look out on the bay.

Site : 7 km S.E. of Mont-Saint-Michel

Next nearest war cemetery :
Saint-James (American) 21 km.

Saint-Désir-de-Lisieux   *Calvados*

3,735 German graves

The cemetery at Saint-Désir in the Pays d'Auge is in open country near a British cemetery. It was set up by the German Army on their withdrawal to the Lower Seine. The greater part of the German soldiers killed in the fighting were interred here by the Commonwealth War Graves personnel. The Volksbund were not concerned with interments but with lay-out and landscape which was carried out between 1957 and 1961. Its 15,000 square metres, make it the smallest of the German cemeteries.

The entrance is through a flat-topped building that gives on the grave-yard against the light, through a semicircular colonnade. Bounded by a hedge-row and planted with big trees like the other German cemeteries, Saint-Désir's distinguishing feature is the beds of Irises at the foot of the head-stones in red sandstone. Each of these have four names inscribed. The tranquility of the place with the green and violet of the Irises in the shade of great trees adds atmosphere and a peculiar light that gives a singular charm to the cemetery.

Site : 2 km west of Lisieux leaving the R.N. 13

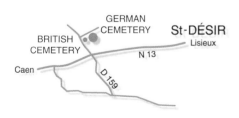

Next nearest war cemetery : Saint-Désir-de-Lisieux (British) a few hundred metres by road.

Champigny-St-André   *Eure*

19,809 German graves

This cemetery was set up during the fighting following the Landings, in the month of August 1944 when Allied Troops advanced towards Paris and the Seine.
The American Graves Service buried here in two great squares of graves, their own soldiers as well as German soldiers.

Behind the entrance building is the commemorative courtyard where large memorial stones have been erected, inscribed with the names of the places from which the victims of war have been transferred. The crosses of the graves are of light conchiferous stone and have names inscribed on both sides with the name, rank, and dates of birth and death of each of those buried on either side. In the 17 squares of unequal size 19,809 German soldiers of the Second World War have been laid to rest. The main alley is paved and leads to the Great Cross of steel, 16 metres high. It can be seen from afar and from all sides of the cemetery, between the squares of graves, near the Ossuary. Here 816 are laid to rest, of which 303 have been identified. The names of those soldiers known are inscribed on stone plaques.

Site : 20 km S.E. of Evreux from Saint-André take the D53 then D72

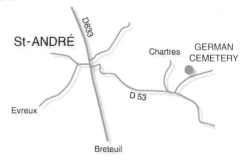

Next nearest war cemeteries : Saint-Désir-de-Lisieux (British & German) 90 km.

A child of destiny

EDMUND
BATON
*19.3.1931 †14.7.1945

As the front line came closer, Edmund BATON, "Lycéen" at Lauterbach (Sarre) was evacuated with his Form in February 1945 to the town of Bad Reichenhall in a safer area. Unknown to his family, Edmund left with one of his school-friends to return home.

Near Stuttgart they had to hide for a whole week because of the fighting. Edmund finally managed to persuade some American soldiers to take them over the Rhine to Strasbourg where the youngsters hoped to catch a train for home. Arriving at the station they were arrested, probably by the French Police and transferred to the other side of France to an internment camp at Poitiers. Edmund BATON died there on 14th July 1945. He was only fourteen.

Mont-d'Huisnes War Cemetery : vault 59, sepulchre 90

"… with great regret… "

Paul RIESSBECK, aged 20 was a pilot and on duty in the Caen area to intercept enemy planes. On 23rd July 1944 his plane, an ME 109 was damaged and he attempted to land in a clearing not far from Chatellier. Just before his aircraft crashed in flames, Paul RIESSBECK jumped. A countryman who saw it happen, took the airman home but could do nothing. Paul RIESSBECK was buried by his comrades near the Church at Chatellier.

In December 1946, his father wrote to the Curé of Chatellier, asking for details about his son's grave. The curé replied as follows :

"Monsieur, I am, with great regret, unable to give you any information about your son, Paul RIESSBECK, I can only confirm that his grave was near the Church until Easter 1945. If memory serves, I believe his name was on one of the crosses. Since Easter 1945 however the body of your son is no longer at Chatellier. At that time, two Americans came and exhumed it, with two of his comrades, buried by his side. On receiving your letter I immediately made further enquiries to find out to where the mortal remains had been transferred, but I have had no answers to my questions. I think that to find where your son's grave is now, you should write to the American Graves Service who are the only people who know. They have laid-out a cemetery, but where ? I do not know."

The American War Graves Commission informed Paul RIESSBECK's father that his son had been transferred at Easter 1945 to the War Cemetery at Champigny-St-André. Paul's brother, Arthur, still visits regularly : grave 1483 in block N° 3.

THE POLISH CEMETERY AT URVILLE

Austere yet moving

This is a cemetery of modest dimensions, rectangular in form, with 696 graves. The make-up is severe, the monuments and crosses are grey. The harsh aspect of these latter give a very austere and military character to the cemetery. The trees, and compact dark-green shrubs confirm this. Many expressions of those visiting the graves of those dear to them, speak, nevertheless of a sense of great intimacy, found at this place of remembrance.

A contemporary character

A paved entrance and double gates in wrought-iron greet the visitor. On gates and railings are rounded iron-work and the arms of eighteen Polish regiments that took part in the Battle of Normandy. The Croix de Guerre and the military medal feature also in the wrought-iron. Facing the entrance, the central alley leads to the far end of the cemetery where a few steps mount up to an altar with a memorial wall behind it, rising almost V-shaped with some polished panels that reflect the light. It forms a vast Cathedral choir, 8 metres high and 13 m 50 across. A statue in aluminium hangs down from it. Stylised, it symbolises the Polish Eagle protecting the fighter. The materials used are very contemporary in concept.

An everyday presence of Kinsfolk

Urville is the only National Polish Cemetery in France. Polish soldiers who fell elsewhere in France have been brought here. By reason of the close links between France and Poland, it is the French Ministry for 'Anciens Combattants' (Veterans) who arranges for the upkeep of this cemetery. Every year a commemoration ceremony is held on the second Sunday in August. Here and there bouquets are placed on graves, a few plaques of remembrance appear near the Altar, Rosaries, at times, are seen hanging on the crosses of graves, as witness that the Polish Community does not forget those of its brethren who died for Freedom.

Site : 17 km south of Caen

Red roses between graves-stones

A row of trimmed evergreens enclose the cemetery on three sides. Yews and Thuyas in front of the gateway contrast sharply with surrounding vegetation. The squares of graves are bordered by Thuyas, from the entrance up to the Altar in front of the Memorial Wall. Tall Poplars silhouette the background against the sky. A Willow has been planted at either end of the line. Fir-Trees form an arc behind the Memorial. Placed at the foot of the tallest, a plaque recalls that they were brought from Poland by three former prisoners of a concentration camp.

Next nearest war cemetery : Cintheaux (Canadian) 5 km.

The work of a Polish committee

The Polish 1st Armoured Division, commanded by Genereal Maczek took part in the fighting which made possible the encirclement and putting to rout of the German Army in Normandy. Engaged at first to the south of Caen near Falaise, Polish Units took part in the fighting at Chambois and Mont Ormel and in the operations that followed around Paris and the North of France.

The cemetery of Urville-Grainville, set up in 1944 by the Commonwealth Graves Commission contains the graves of 569 Polish soldiers. In 1950, 127 soldiers buried in various French churchyards were transferred to Urville. In April 1951 the British who up to that time had maintained it, passed it to the French Authorities. The Polish Veterans Mutual Association, based in Potigny then took charge of looking after the graves.

This society in 1952 passed on the work to the "Comité du Cimetière Polonais d'Urville" which, with the help of the Caen architect, Pierre Bienvenu little by little laid-out and embellished the cemetery until 1960. Thanks to a subscription raised and gifts received a monument in memory of the soldiers was erected in 1954.

In 1961 the committee considered that : "the Polish Combattants had been given a sepulchre worthy of their sacrifice" and handed back the cemetery to "Le Service Français des Sépultures des Anciens Combattants." The last touch, added in 1971 was the placing of the arms of the Polish Units on the entrance wrought-iron grille by the Old Comrades Association of the 1st D.B.

THE FRENCH NATIONAL WAR CEMETERY AT RADON - LES GATEYS

From Africa to Berchtesgaden

In 1943 having fought in Africa, the French 2nd Armoured Division commanded by General Leclerc, joined the American XV Corps, under the orders of General Patton. On 12th August 1944, General Leclerc penetrated Alençon. With the aid of the Maquis, he moved in and surrounded the Forêt d'Écouves to cut the road to Paris and liberate Échouché. 2nd French Armoured then fought its way to Paris, then Strasbourg, then in Germany to stop at Berchtesgaden.

Most of the French soldiers in 2nd French Armoured who fell during the Battle of Normandy lie near their families. Those who repose in the Forêt d'Écouves are nineteen soldiers transferred from neighbouring churchyards. This French War Cemetery was set up in 1970 at the request of "L'Association des Anciens de la 2de D.B." (2nd Armoured Old Comrades Association). It was inaugurated on 15th March of the same year in the presence of Madame la Maréchale Leclerc and General Massu. In 1989, its maintenance was handed over to the "Service Français des Sépultures des Anciens Combattants" who carried out the present lay-out.

This cemetery discreetly laid-out has an air of great calm. The few visitors who come in cannot fail to sense the majesty of the place. All the emotion that surges up, in this place of rest lies hidden under the great Beeches.

On the edge of the Forêt d'Écouves

In the Municipality of Saint-Nicolas-des-Bois, this cemetery lies away from the main roads. It is not far from Radon, on the edge of the magnificent Forêt d'Écouves. It is small in size, since it contains only seventeen graves in which lie nineteen soldiers.

At the entrance a low wall flanks two pillars of Vosges sandstone between which are double gates of wrought-iron each of which incorporate a Croix-de-Guerre. The two rows of grave-stones are set in a square, bounded by a border of stone. The headstones are all beige in colour but differ in form respecting the origin and diversity of the combattants in 2nd Armoured Division. Twelve of them have Latin Crosses, four others have stones of oriental type inscribed with the Star and Crescent. The last head-stone, rectangular and rounded at the top is inscribed with the Star of David. Each stone gives the Name, Unit and the Date and Place where each soldier fell. All carry the inscription : "Mort pour la France" and the famous badge of 2nd French Armoured Division. An oblique plaque in black stone honours sixty-nine who died in 2nd French Armoured. A ceremony takes place every year here on 12th August, the Anniversary date of the Liberation of Alençon and the surrounding country.

Site : 8 km north of Alençon on the D26

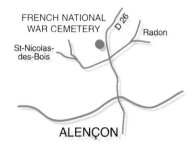

Next nearest war cemetery :
Grainville - Langannerie (Polish) 80 km

Veritable gardens…

Respect for the Dead constitutes a notion inherent in every liberal and democratic society. It recognises the inestimable price of life. The last two world wars have sharpened our consciences in these values. The Treaty of Versailles established the right of a grave for every soldier. But if every man is honoured individually, it is collectively a desire to make these war cemeteries places of remembrance and historic conscience.

A sense of the aesthetic and the artistic are joined in surpassing the horrors of war, to symbolise sacrifice and Peace regained. In the concept of a garden each graveyard retains the last tangible traces of the fighting. The essential element in the cemeteries is vegetation. It seems, like hope to spring eternal and by its myriad variations through the seasons to bring life to these gardens of remembrance.

… where one cannot forget

Every nation knew how to give them a different soul, a direct expression of its culture. The visitor knows at first sight in which country he is. American cemeteries are vast and majestic parks. Commonwealth cemeteries, more numerous are so many little gardens with hedges and flowers. German cemeteries whilst blending into the countryside present an image that is strong and laid bare. National grave-yards with an emotional aspect are perhaps the most military.

Born of a collective conscience, war cemeteries have been set up so that the living may come there to meditate and remember. Over and above official commemorations, a private visit to these places brings back all the atrocity of war. Emotion makes for better understanding than words, the message contained forever in the tombs.